EXPLORING PSALMANAZAR

EXPLORING PSALMANAZAR

JOHN GOHORRY

Shoestring Press

All rights reserved. No part of this work covered by the copyright herein may be reproduced or used in any means—graphic, electronic, or mechanical, including copying, recording, taping, or information storage and retrieval systems—without written permission of the publisher.

Printed by imprintdigital
Upton Pyne, Exeter
www.digital.imprint.co.uk

Typesetting and cover design by narrator
www.narrator.me.uk
info@narrator.me.uk
033 022 300 39

Published by Shoestring Press
19 Devonshire Avenue, Beeston, Nottingham, NG9 1BS
(0115) 925 1827
www.shoestringpress.co.uk

First published 2020
© Copyright: John Gohorry
© Cover image: Stoecklein *Map of Taiwan or Formosa and Fujian, China, 1726* (recreated by narrator)

The moral right of the author has been asserted.

ISBN 978-1-912524-21-1

ACKNOWLEDGEMENTS

V *Fallacy of the doorkeepers* (TLS, 6 January 1995)

IV *An invented man*, VIII *The birth of language* and IX *Birds* (Stand Vol 16 no 4, 2018)

For Gerlinde

CONTENTS

Exploring Psalmanazar: an introduction   1

I	Walking away from the obvious	7
II	Midst	9
III	A shipwreck	10
IV	An invented man	12
V	Fallacy of the doorkeepers	14
VI	Travelling through the red towns	16
VII	Table talk	18
VIII	The birth of language	20
IX	Birds	21
X	Inventing Formosa	22
XI	Selves	25
XII	A man of no rank	27
XIII	Imagining East	29
XIV	Three versions of autobiography	30
XV	The maze	33
XVI	Craft	36
XVII	Persistent, resourceful, pragmatic	38
XVIII	Ritualle	40
XIX	Three glimpses of Oku	41
XX	Vincere potere	42
XXI	One version of Cicero	43
XXII	Babelbabble	45
XXIII	Another version of Cicero	46
XXIV	A partnership, then	48
XXV	Ulterior motives	49
XXVI	Ulterior motives (ii)	50
XXVII	In the Erasmusstad	51
XXVIII	Nullius in verba	52
XXIX	Chimneys	53
XXX	Tonguetwisters	54
XXXI	At Eden-on-Thames	56
XXXII	At a Christ Church dinner	57
XXXIII	The art of fiction	58
XXXIV	Postverital (i) Silk	60

XXXV	Postverital	(ii) Two verbs from Formosa	63
XXXVI	Postverital	(iii) Bamboo	65
XXXVII	Postverital	(iv) The Maxim of Affirmation	68
XXXVIII	De libro suo		70
XXXIX	Inventions		72
XL	A discourse from servitude		73
XLI	A fan shop, 1717		75
XLII	Autobiography, 2017		77
XLIII	Breathing space		81
XLIV	Disengagement		82
XLV	Mastering Hebrew		83
XLVI	The Antichthon expedition		85
XLVII	Intimations		87
XLVIII	Managing history		88
XLIX	Three women		89
L	Laudanum		91
LI	An internet journey		93
LII	Inheritance		95

EXPLORING PSALMANAZAR: AN INTRODUCTION

I first became aware of George Psalmanazar in the mid 1960's when I was spending time in the British Library, still situated at that time within the precincts of the British Museum. I was there ostensibly to work on an M.Phil. thesis on Sidney's *Arcadia,* which I eventually completed in 1970, but I found the atmosphere and the resources of the Reading Room, and to a lesser extent those of the North Library, highly conducive to the practice of digressive enquiry, so much so that on several occasions, progress on my main project ran serious risk of foundering. I saw myself, not unrealistically, in a place like the one Borges describes in *The Library of Babel*—an environment characterised by a marked symmetry of design (a vast circular space, surmounted by a dome, with shelves, galleries, branching corridors), the shelf marks of its books and its enormous accessions catalogue implying proliferation and enlargement, a breathing, infinitely expanding universe of criticism and creation amplified even in the writings of those like myself who came to work at its desks, and giving the individual imagination no alternative but to pursue such enquiries as aroused its curiosity. I was able to pursue many avenues of interest, among them the phenomenon of George Psalmanazar.

The library contained two books by Psalmanazar, and I read and made notes on them both. Their title pages are worth quoting in full. The first was published in 1704, the year after he arrived in England. He is thought to have been about 25 at the time. The title page reads as follows:-

> AN HISTORICAL and GEOGRAPHICAL DESCRIPTION OF FORMOSA, AN Island subject to the Emperor of JAPAN, GIVING An Account of the Religion, Customs, Manner *etc* of the Inhabitants. Together with a Relation of what happen'd to the Author in his Travels; particularly his Conferences with the *Jesuits*, and others, in several Parts of *Europe*. Also the History and Reasons of his Conversion to

Christianity, with his Objections against it (in defence of Paganism) and their Answers. To which is prefix'd, A PREFACE in Vindication of himself from the Reflections of a *Jesuit* lately come from *China*, with an Account of what passed between them. By GEORGE PSALMANAAZAAR, a Native of the said Island, now in *London*. Illustrated with several Cuts. *LONDON:* Printed for *Dan. Brown*, at the *Black Swan* without *Temple-Bar*; *G. Strahan* and *W. Davis*, in *Cornhill*; and *Fran. Coggan*, in the *Inner-Temple-Lane* 1704.

The second was published in 1764, the year after he died. The title page reads:-

MEMOIRS of ****, Commonly known by the name of GEORGE PSALMANAZAR; A Reputed Native of FORMOSA. Written by himself In order to be published after his Death. CONTAINING An Account of his Education, Travels, Adventures, Connections, Literary Productions, and pretended Conversion from Heathenism to Christianity, which last proved the Occasion of his being brought over into this Kingdom, and passing for a Proselyte, and a Member of the Church of England. LONDON: PRINTED FOR THE EXECUTRIX. Sold by R.DAVIS, in Picadilly; J.NEWBERY, in St. Paul's Church-Yard; L.DAVIS, and C.REYMERS in Holborn. MDCCLXIV.

The two books mark the beginning and the end of Psalmanazar's literary life and career in England; he began by passing himself off as a native of a country he had never visited, and embroidered the very little that was known about that country at the time with a wealth of invented historical, geographical, social and cultural detail that was so coherent as to be taken as authentic by many, perhaps most, of the English intelligentsia, including Bishops of the Church of England and members of the Royal Society. He ended it by leaving his executrix a confessional manuscript which repudiates his deception, offers frequent affirmations of his repentance and his

Christian faith, and gives a fuller and more truthful account of his life, including his addiction to laudanum, his contribution to various works of historical scholarship, and his long and successful apprenticeship learning Hebrew.

There was a strong imaginative discharge for me from both of these books. From the outset I was drawn to Psalmanazar's account of the Formosan language—it was a forged language, but one that he was able to speak fluently; it had an alphabet, names for numbers and for the months, and a vocabulary that enabled him to translate Christian texts (the Lord's Prayer, the Apostles' Creed, and the Ten Commandments are given in dual language versions). It had a grammar; it was, as Barbara Strang has defined language, 'an articulated system of signs.'

If the first book was grounded in falsehoods that had a strong aura of authenticity about them, the second book was grounded in truths that in spite of everything carried more than a suspicion of falsehood. I found it very difficult to discredit the sincerity of Psalmanazar's repentance, but I found it odd in the extreme that at no point in this document of disclosure did he declare his true name, or his precise origins such as the name of the town where he was actually born, or the names of his parents. Even the will which he wrote first on 23 April 1752 Old Style, which he ratified and confirmed, unchanged, on 1 January ten years later (four months before his death), and which was prefixed to the *Memoirs*, was issued as 'THE LAST WILL AND TESTAMENT OF ME A POOR SINFUL AND WORTHLESS CREATURE COMMONLY KNOWN BY THE ASSUMED NAME OF GEORGE PSALMANAZAR.' And why did he wait until he was dead for the publication of his narrative of repentance? He states in his will that a posthumous work 'would be less liable to suspicion, as the author would be far out of the influence of any sinister motives that might induce him to deviate from the truth.' I couldn't myself see that postponing publication of a document until after one's death would have any bearing on the truth of what the author put in it. Indeed, deferring publication until after one's death might be a way of avoiding the argumentative consequences of having been selective in the truths that one wrote, or indeed of having set down some things which were in fact untrue.

I began to suspect that to look at Psalmanazar's work in terms of a straightforward binary opposition between falsehood (the *Description of Formosa*) and truth (the *Memoirs*) was an oversimplification, but I struggled to identify an alternative. I left London in 1971; other concerns took over, and in wasn't until 1994 that the completion of my Samuel Johnson poems took me back to thinking about Psalmanazar and picking up my notes. Between January and November of that year I drafted a number of poems arising out of the tensions between truth and falsehood in my readings of those two books, discovering as I did so that what informed them was not primarily cognitive, but imaginative activity, that is, the dynamic proliferation of enquiring mind through all the resources that come to it, or that it can lay itself open to, in a bid to create satisfactory (i.e. pleasing) aesthetic relations. By the November of 1994 I had exhausted my energies and my resources (my notes) so I laid Psalmanazar aside once again and got on with other things.

It was April 2015 by the time I resumed work on the sequence, a process greatly facilitated by two developments that had occurred in the interval. One was the publication (in 2004) of Michael Keevak's *The Pretended Asian—George Psalmanazar's Eighteenth-Century Formosan Hoax*; the other was the greatly enhanced access to both primary and secondary sources of information that had come about through the internet. There were digital versions of Psalmanazar's books, and a raft of associated documents that enabled me to follow up all the threads and tributaries of enquiry that suggested themselves.

As I say, I felt from the outset that there was something within the writings of Psalmanazar that went beyond a simple narrative of a Formosan hoax that its perpetrator came in later life to confess and to repudiate. There is, I came to realise, a profound continuity between the early and the late Psalmanazar, and it lies in his preoccupation with the two languages (other than the Latin, English and presumably the French he used for everyday purposes) that featured so prominently among his concerns—the Formosan he invented, and the Hebrew which he learned.

The later parts of the *Memoirs* contain a good deal about how Psalmanazar set about learning Hebrew—not that he was completely ignorant of it when it came to inventing Formosan—the names and letter forms of some, though not all, of the letters in his alphabet show clear affinities with Hebrew models. His account tells of his moving away from reading Hebrew grammar books to immersing himself in Hebrew translations of Latin versions of the Psalms, and his acquiring a grasp of both vocabulary and grammar through this process of attentive immersion. The process enabled him in due course to read most of the Old Testament books in Hebrew (and from this to contribute a *History of the Jews* to Volume VII of the *Universal History*) and to speak Hebrew with some of the Moroccan Jews worshipping at the Bevis Marks Synagogue in the City of London.

Attentive immersion is of course another aspect of what I earlier called the dynamic proliferation of enquiring mind, and what I refer to in one of the poems in the sequence as *bamboo mind*. Both aspects are as applicable to the making of poems as they are to the learning (or the invention) of languages, and given that Psalmanazar's books offer two different versions of his autobiography (each of them marked by judicious omissions) I felt no necessity to choose between them but instead grounded my poems in whatever elements of either version, and indeed of my own life, offered creative opportunities. *Exploring Psalmanazar* therefore is a title that points both to a profound characteristic of my subject—Psalmanazar was a resourceful, courageous, and adventurous explorer of the possibilities of human language—and to the investigative impetus behind the poems themselves.

John Gohorry
Letchworth Garden City, April 2017

I *WALKING AWAY FROM THE OBVIOUS*

This was your masterstroke.
You drafted yourself into a maze
that admitted so many solutions
you became your desired enigma.

Each track to your imagined centre
was its plausible narrative,
a chronicle of the seven ages
that drew a blank, faced a brick wall.

Ambition, connivance, deception,
the sweet smoke of regard,
then obscurity, then repentance,
and the regular, measured decades

that turned history as precisely
as a carpenter working his lathe
—these were themselves a fable
for your inquisitor to examine

and draw a preferred conclusion
whether his own or their author's.
In the long reach of imagining
I anticipate substance and style

needing, beyond an entrance,
to find the right passageway,
whether deliberative or forensic,
into the human heart

but cross-purposed at every turn
by the logics of self-denial
you drew from your experience
find my way is obstructed

by such moving conformities
that in spite of my love of truth
I would wish to validate them.
What shall I say to you then,

an equally flawed man from a later,
less moral age, when I set my light
to a course that your last record
would hold wrong or devious?

Only that each of us must begin
from his own starting place, taking
one step at a time, treading carefully
a path that his judgement suggests

will neither collapse under his feet
nor lead him to error. And sometimes
knowing only that what is self-evident
may be self-destructive, walks from it

through falsehood, even as you did,
only the step that circumvents, mounts,
or breaks through the face of the wall,
like this text, worth having confidence in.

II *MIDST*

In the midst of the real, the myth
in the midst of the myth, the real.

III *A SHIPWRECK*

A man in his externalities,
breathes desire, fear, languages.

More distant than Antichthon,
fabled Atlantis, or the lands of Zen

is the envisaged shore
where baboons scream and gesture

as the *Harwich* goes down
and macaws shriek their commentary

flying in and out of the camphor laurels.
Friends, what country is this? Understand

the supposing sense growing accustomed
to its own laws of direction, and strengthening

one day after another as its particular
apprehensions figure themselves in the texture

of the event, where as performer and witness
you immerse yourself in the relation of images,

each text a grained print developed by your art
and concerned with its authenticity

when proof only is correspondence, and you,
hitherto the invisible man, must walk out of the shade

and present some less composed face
to whoever wants to examine it.

Some distance inland, grammars are formed,
vocabularies dreamed one day to be reckoned with,

their mumbo nominatives as wholly adequate
as perhaps later Volapuk, Esperanto

to report how turtles floated like clouds
in the soutanes of the wrecked missionaries

and the baboons sensing tragedy, not to be harmed,
busied themselves, perhaps truly indifferent.

IV *AN INVENTED MAN*

Let a man be invented as a poem is,
or as his discourse, of which on a day

void of surprises he imagines himself
both origin and director; let him find

himself drafted, revised, questioned,
challenged and re-formed to the least

phrase of his being, which at its best
(its most stubborn, its most articulate)

conforms thought and word in a figure
that, being neither, at once unites both

in the same substance of brain and finger
from which he is himself manipulated;

and let him step sideways from all rhetorics
that elaborate fact to rococo travesties

of what is the case, or the gaudy fabrics
of a conceit that is merely fashionable;

then he will understand he is governed
by the same laws that rule all invention

and since he is fiction, reach after truth
not as transcribers but as conjurors do,

each pass of the hand folding illusion
into illusion so surely that disbelief

surrenders herself in a new act of naming,
and probabilities long since unsuspected,

wake from their sleep in the folds of what
may be the case to grow bold and vigorous;

consistent, and so believed; full of grace,
and so giving delight even as they instruct;

artless, as his tongue that pronounced them
valid; and truthful, as they conformed to truth.

V FALLACY OF THE DOORKEEPERS

One doorkeeper always deceives.
The other is always truthful.

You can resolve the conundrum
by framing the right question.

If I were to ask your companion
which door leads to the treasure

what would his answer be?
You then choose the other.

But *always* itself is fallacious.
The golden-tongued doorkeeper,

growing sullen, calls iron down
to give strength to his fabling days,

his austerities tongue-in-cheek
when they are not deadpan, and so

always hard to interpret; his partner,
growing adventurous, ties a twist

in habitual fact as one might improvise
rabbits from handkerchiefs, or project

onto a wall familiar or fabled beasts
made out of finger-shadows, truth

which had once seemed self-evident
wrapped now in Cretan complexities

becoming at best comical or grotesque;
at worst, too obscure for admission.

How then shall we know anything other
than what is tautologous for certain?

or pass through a thousand doorways
expecting whatever lies on the far side

to acquiesce in our *is or is not the case*?
Are doorkeepers not also husbands, wives?

Can we be creatures of fact, inventing lives?
Building fables, be other than fabulous?

VI *TRAVELLING THROUGH THE RED TOWNS*

Remember the red towns between Turin and Avignon,
the carts lurching out of the distance towards you
grinding past to the wild song of a particular axle,

the roadsides all day oppressive under a fierce sun
and the thick smell of nothing at all happening. Days
weigh you in their undifferentiated, impalpable hours

as you might yourself weigh some small roadside stone
before tossing it into the hedgerow, or look for some
distinguishing mark, some blemish, some lucky sign,

that slipping it into a pocket, you might be protected.
These men driving their carts are not your father,
and not your mother those women, black-backed

in the gatherings of a distant field, though too far off
to ignore or respond were you to call them mother.
Still you improvise and elaborate on the dull day,

a man that must take whatever he lays his hands on
and make with it what music he can, its frustrations,
disappointments, deferrals giving rise to a litany

of names and not-names that, once used, grow authentic,
Gafre, Salcurie, Nunques, Bourg d'Oisans, Bille,
Moucheville, Modane, Etangs, Estevat-les-Guiches,

towns resonant with the suffused magic of memory
and invention, as in these hours of increasing distance
from the low hamlet you celebrate as your birthplace

with the wind's discourse in the trees. Here is a great
stone house with windows and flagged courtyards,
where behind wrought-iron gateways tutors patrol,

their thoughts busy with Virgil, their pupil's grasp
of accusative and infinitive or the fourth declension;
here under an oak a girl in a red bonnet orchestrates

a huddle of under-fives in their afternoon playschool
singing *Jolietment*, while from the cloister opposite
the burden of plainsong lifts into the vault of the nave

overrunning with praise to dissolve in its own echoes.
In this part of the world speech is operatic, theatrical,
and conventions of soliloquy always strictly observed

so that performance, not utterance, is what's normal,
and every exchange, already fully rehearsed, is only
the most recent trial of a discourse that, given chance

and a critical ear, may one day be definitive. Anyhow,
everything, as you know, is constantly underpinned,
sustained and informed by the tremor of improvisation

we crystallise into sense, truth, the orthodox wisdom
we assign value, significance to, as at this late hour
we detain passers by with the tenth draft of a fiction

to give street credibility to our begging. As day closes
we examine the plot carefully where we are to sleep
and write out into the great book which is our mind

a stave invention shaped and redefined, untruth that
passed for, and, as the book would have it, surpassed
truth, all those remembered towns we travelled through.

VII *TABLE TALK*

A preference for abstract language,
analogies, the scholarly passive. These,
you imagine, hearing authorities cited,
are sure signs of philosophers talking

as those of lovers are languid silences
in which all thought construes sense
of its other in a progressive reflex,
each gesture the innocent conjugation

of some new aspect of the verb *to love*
unrecognised in the world's paraphrase
until hands touched or eyes glanced,
or at another table gamblers reckoned

share prices might fall, the black mare
gallop first over the line, a heart win.
But today, as you bring coffee, wine,
a discreet solicitude to the cafe tables,

you overhear the argument from design
deployed amid oaths, a rough emphasis
of gamblers' discourse; lovers discuss
effect, probability, rational advantage,

and, though the day is fine, betting men,
taking no chances, carry umbrellas.
Thus it seems occupation, personality
are subsumed in the music of utterance

that creates and informs them, gambler,
lover, philosopher being no longer persons
but descriptions of discourse, yourself
also attendant to the same contingencies

as to the tables you serve. What matters,
it seems, is not that we should correspond
to ourselves, but that we forge discourse,
its song rising above truth, wisdom, folly,

bluff, gossip, fact, counterfeit, daydream,
fiction, falsehood, deception, all the regular
trades we do business in, to defy habit,
our excellent service being to propagate

a blue line of imagining over the boundary
of all that was ever known, to interrogate
and convict—and so, to prolong life. Set
the bill down on the tablecloth, wait while

the small change is tipped onto the saucer,
and rather than be yourself, be the history
that occasion presents. Customers leave,
each point and tempo of their departure

a carefully-judged caesura that balances
hint, argument and prediction, antecedent
agenda, with various modes of acceptance
that remain to be sealed walking away

in a flawless performance that perfectly
confounds truth, falsehood's counterfeit,
in a being that you, constant witness to love,
fate, probability, know now for your own.

VIII *THE BIRTH OF LANGUAGE*

From the cliff of your brow, gulls soared
into unqualified space.

Fish slipped through the dappled shade
of your rib shallows.

So metaphor cross-dressed thought,
and the woman who was the island

from the groyne to the broad headland
stretched her torso of sand.

Each vowel grew incandescent
in the furnace of observation,

its distinct cry tumultuous
as the throat that supported the cliff,

as the grain of the skin shivering
at the gulls' scream overhead.

IX *BIRDS*

For some reason, you keep thinking of birds.
This morning, a hawk hung in your mind's eye,
its vigilance the harangue of the object.

When sparrows burst out of the undergrowth
in a flurry of wings, you were bird-brained,
imagining refuges, branches of argument

in which even now rooks coil and resettle
as the wind disallows certainties. So perhaps talk
is best understood as a species of bird flight,

that sudden parabola, thought arching upward
in the wake of invention, that regular pulse,
the fictive heart quickening like yours into song.

X INVENTING FORMOSA

You serve, and you are attentive.
This is the first obligation
both of waiter at table and poet

whose arts are engendered not
in self-clamour, the ego's greed
for its own gratification,

but (though sometimes performance
convert to a sociable rapture)
to self-effacement, concealment,

the assertive mind being suspended
in a stillness of observation
kept from narrative as from disclosure

in an archive between the ears
which memory often visits
and the vein of imagination

bringing dimension and colour
shapes to its own likenesses.
Thus, witnessing so many evenings

the way discourse enlarges itself
into hoodwink, exaggeration,
a mere pinch of palpable untruth

fingered over their conversation
giving savour to narrative,
and to persuasive thought

a lustre not shared by ungarnished
facts, you also choose to dissemble,
not augmenting the subject of talk

with a burden of fable, a chronicle
of abstractions that, later perhaps,
may be reinvented as allegory

but engendering talk itself, first
a trickle of light syllables
running over the hillside stones,

bright voices suggesting an alphabet
never before heard by these ears
and the blows of an axe falling

in some remote forest clearing
where a naked man labours
and each fraction of uncoiled effort

conceiving between each upward heft
and each downward heave of the blade
a fresh ordinal, comprehends number

and as night blackens the laurels
sums each individual stroke
in the crash of his felled tree.

Thus you make a reckoning not
in the regular *Een, zwee, dree*
but in *tauf, bogio, charhe,*

terms only the dance of the pen
and the gleam of the right change
render intelligible, and *Good night*

is a *Va hem shemona* courtesy
conjured out of that fictive darkness,
played with one syllable at a time

over the coffee cups and hence now
in civilities of repeated exchange
makes occasion to be authentic.

What begins is compression of sense,
a nexus of breath and stop
that configures the spirit's ether

to the vision it apprehends
and envisages as it pronounces
the word only by which mind

drives to what may be thought
and side by side with the known
accommodates all you dream.

Closing up for the night, your mind
is a pool green with imaginings,
a saturated solution where crystal

begins magical growth, the unspoken
condensing substance, flesh, lexis
about its bare runes. Somewhere,

a star explodes You notice the flare
only as it is extinguished. You know
no word for this in any familiar tongue.

XI *SELVES*

You imagine those fictive selves
shells of the man you are;

generous and courageous
they crowd out your imperfections

with endurance and money
or unravel the tangled fact

in its skein of circumstance
with more care and economy

than you could ever muster.
Or like those killjoys mouthing

home truths as the music blares
and just as the Certificate

of Authentic Achievement settles
into your grasp, mutter darkly,

*Don't for one instant mistake
this charade for the real thing*

*which is beyond your reach
if it exists at all, and if it does not*

only conspires to delude you.
Think of them, dexter, sinister,

light brigade, awkward squad,
as companions and opposites

whose gift is to fashion you
into depth, certain proportion

as, crazed, single-mindedly now
they spring to life, imagining you.

XII A MAN OF NO RANK

At the foot of the hill that morning
you did not see Noviomage.

Nor did you meet him later
(neither by accident nor design)

in town gardens you both frequent
or at *The Contemplatives* restaurant

where you thought you might share
a side table, a few wise words.

When, later, you called at his house,
he was out, neighbours reported,

reaching towards his thought
on the far side of the mountain

neither expected back nor presumed
to have abandoned old habits.

In speaking of him to others
you use only negation,

an affirmative coil snaking
beyond, to the side, falling short

of a figure that moves steadily
through the icons of language

and without hope or regret
empties each present moment

whole into his vessel of silence
and will speak when you next meet

of cloud, birdsong, that drift
of trees rounding the foot of the hill.

XIII *IMAGINING EAST*

All this talk of belonging, of not belonging.
The mind, eager to solve an enigma, flies
after judgement, distinction, lost causes,
to define itself *per genus et differentiam*.

Or as neither body nor soul. What aspires,
urges, desires, cogitates in its own reflex
(or the mind of another) breeds difference
as it endures growth, season, vicissitude.

Thus parentheses close. Mind settles back
into its fastness, imagining east, countries
fragrant with blossom of petalled languages,
hill slopes, a falling tone that does not deceive.

XIV THREE VERSIONS OF AUTOBIOGRAPHY

(i)

I was born, declares one of the doorkeepers
(discreet still, even in disclosure)
on the road between Rome and Avignon.

My soul spoke the language of grasshoppers,
palaver of linnet and song-thrush
until strengthened with paternosters

I gypsied the roads to the far north
living off roots and berries;
what I sought was my skeined father

by whom alone I might reach the domed
plenitude most speak of as salvation.
Trust the inscription over this doorway,

for none pass but those faithful to what
truly happened, and the clear fact fixed
in performance none can return to change.

(ii)

Every evening she murmured those secret words
you remembered being spoken of as *The nice things*
though the doorkeeper recalled only fragments

lodged like crystal seeds in the back of his mind
that grew about certain declensions, prayers, rhythmic
chants, certain readings and listenings, confederations

of talk nourished underneath ceilings, in gardens
where fires burned, a ditch flooded, and underground
autumn's stalks mouldered like the imagined dead.

These grounded his *ur-Gebiet*, the imagined lands
perfectly known before they were quite forgotten,
the continent he set out that very day to discover

and spent his life in pursuit of. Each minute swung
on its hinges of fact. You pushed open this door
to the schemed lives others spoke of as fiction.

(iii)

I was born, therefore, in Externitsa,
runs the last draft of the doorkeeper's narrative,
eldest and loved son of a prosperous merchant.

In glades loud with macaws, my tutor
schooled me to the right use of a final clause,
the right working of oratio obliqua

though his instances pro and contra concealed
Jesuit artifice, working me into the nets
of his faith by example and sorites.

Yet he spoke to me of green lands where men
in great houses read nature's book, fracturing
light on surfaces cracked open to new knowledge.

My ghostly father. As Aeneas dreamed
of the high walls he must found, setting out
from his ruined origin over a wide sea,

so I fled ten thousand leagues, breaking out
in a frail boat, stowaway to a fable
once having arrived at I should know for truth.

And this I present you, authentic, unedited
but for some trifles of accident, leaving events
uncompromised by artifice, exactly as they occurred.

Thus the doorkeeper's chronicle. You read carefully,
walking a tightrope hung from falsehood to falsehood
integral to the fiction, diligent after the truth.

XV THE MAZE

On the far side of that doorway
you discovered a labyrinth.

Each wall ranged its solid belief
on a massy foundation, square

to the aperture you must pass through,
each act of assent reaching for truth

at some ultimate centre, though
blind alleys should close about you

and error grow your familiar.
Did the divine concede limit

that one drown of the shipwrecked five
yielding to nature what its power

could not aggregate? Was the god
capable only in part? strong

only as currents permitted,
himself tidelike in flow and ebb?

Suppose all believers alike
and faith's ground common to all

yielding all hope of survival;
did the event nonsuit belief

to leave expectation agape
in the prayers that supported it

as it slipped into the sea's throat
down each fathom of its denial?

Perhaps the god, seeing beyond faith
glimpsed differing antecedents

and so shaped his different judgements,
survival or drowning the just

merit of those that survived or drowned
and each fate tempered with mercy

in fact, as it rewarded faith
with the sight of what grounded it.

You imagined the still centre,
the aloof core you reached towards,

its secret concealed by the rise
of the walls still perplexing you

at each reasoned affirmation
that even as you thought to approach

shielded you from it. You found thought
treacherous as your own footstep,

words solid, resistant as stone
to the service you asked of them,

locked in their familiar prisons
of designation and purpose

the sign of the thought of the thing
that, being other, eluded you.

What, then, should deliver the word
but speech resonant with the cry

of sea birds, gabble of monkeys,
a vigorous, alien discourse

the lift of whose intonations
cousined Babels and Avagais

in a zen shout that confounded
the labyrinth of thought's direction

and in the Jericho silence
broke open your figured quatrain

that neither denied nor deferred
the heart beating its rough measures

but skilled only in truth's service
unravelled the skein of a song

the illusory world concealed
in its qualified utterance

yet selfless melodic witness
should draw through the heart of the maze.

XVI *CRAFT*

In zazen, the word *craft* keeps occurring.
You neither welcome nor ban it, but notice
it as it creeps, ivy-like, round your heart.

It enters your veins and circulates
at the pulse rate your breathing has slowed
to—what?—twenty five beats a minute.

You envisage it sometimes as a vessel,
a solid clinker-built skiff or wherry
of four consonants and a vowel

pushing its prow with or against
the currents of what you're imagining
as you reach towards empty mind.

Today, it's a coracle, turning about
and about as it finds a way downstream
surrendering itself so completely,

it seems, to the forces that drive it
as to be wholly without guile. Where
is control? Where direction? Yet it reaches

the point where, so to speak, it wants
to be, which is none other than the place
where it is. Is it by this, or some other means

that *craft* comes to signify *cunning,*
agile mind's capability to mask truth
in a stealthcoat of seeming so artfully worn

as to be judged authentic? Perhaps,
beneath spindrift of circumstance, there is
always directing mind—sly, subtle,

deceptive / deliberate, artful not only
in wearing the coat but in spinning its very fabric,
craft being an art of contriving. So mind floods,

drains and floods again with cognition's debris,
sensation, image, reflection, the vague germ
of some scheme of contriving not to be stilled

by a slab of imagined butter placed
on the crown of your head and let trickle
over your ears, cheeks, chin, shoulders,

the cliffs of your back and your abdomen
onto groin, haunches and ankles. Outside
in the Rue St Denis, the world's traffic

goes on, does a roaring trade, with pimps,
whores, barrowboys bawling their wares
to whoever goes by, but here in your room

you cultivate stillness, imagine yourself
on Hansho, in Hara and a drop at a time
water the *nen* of devising, give nothing away.

XVII *PERSISTENT, RESOURCEFUL, PRAGMATIC*

You yourself can't remember
how long you patrolled the maze
before finding the tiny space
between doctrine and doctrine
just wide enough to squeeze through.

Certainly you have lost weight
working your way round and round,
knocking on doors, on barred shutters,
begging a crust where you can.
Famished and no doubt delirious,

you come to the gap in daylight
(it's no more than a crevice)
where freeing your lungs of air
as one might passing a midden
you heave yourself suddenly through.

Before you a great city shimmers
in the afternoon sunlight, far off
across a broad plain set with tents,
banners, pavilions. Clouds of dust
rise from the hooves of horses,

the cavalry lines of an army
drawn and re-drawing themselves
into fresh formations; heavy
artillery thumps in the distance
and as you approach you can see

groups of infantry marching,
the regular, four-beats-to-a-bar
tread of parade-ground battalions.
Neither allegory nor mirage,
what you see gives you the hope

of a square meal and a fresh start.
And now the recruiting sergeant
signs you up to the regiment,
space to confound what you are
in the guile of your new calling.

XVIII *RITUALLE*

Kneeling to face the sunset
you sprinkle your hair with water
and chant *Ornio basta hamari;
basta Ornio hamari gastun,*
gesture and word alike signalling
due worship, respect and honour.

You retire to your chair, and wrapped
in a shawl snore night away upright.
You rise with the sun, sprinkle your hair

again, kneel facing the east
and pray *Vomera, Ornio, vomera,
gastun Ornio mova tostavomera.*

Public professions of difference
provoke mirth or astonishment
as you intend they should — preludes,
you hope, to enquiry, to argument,
finally, to acceptance, the shared
space that would make you legitimate.

XIX   THREE GLIMPSES OF OKU

Your breakfast is raw beef flavoured
with cardamom seeds. Private Wolters
can hardly believe his eyes.

But on Oku, you tell him,
people breakfast on snakes, mice, human brains
uncooked, parcelled in seaweed.

You wear lipstick, mascara, streak
your forehead with henna. Private Hendricks
is covered with admiration.

But on Oku, you tell him,
men's bodies are fields of flowers,
all painted at once, like rainbows.

You disbelieve Wolters' tale
of a woman in Amsterdam giving birth
to quintuplets at forty.

Though on Oku, you tell him, *a woman
may conceive at a hundred and twenty.
A man is still young at two hundred.*

Wolters is learning Mumblespeak
—a few words of greeting and gratitude.
Cholty Cholt first thing in the morning,

Tohai when asking a favour. *Tomahai*
when granting one. Hendricks has not yet
dared ask what's Oku for *Bullshit*.

XX *VINCERE POTERE*

In the land of *What if*
anything's possible.

Indicative is subjunctive
as it never were.

XXI ONE VERSION OF CICERO

The man dressed as chaplain has his suspicions
and moreover, a plan to test them.

Put this into Japanese, he invites you, offering
Cicero *De Officiis* 1.18:-

Ex quattuor autem locis	*[Now of the four parts*
in quos honesti	*into which we have divided*
naturam vimque divisimus,	*the notion of moral goodness,*
primus ille	*the first,*
qui in veri cognitione consistit	*which consists in the knowledge of truth, touches*
maxime naturam attingit humanam.	*human nature most closely.]*

You frown. The translation must not seem too easy.
Fy raevvaus eavin mudat, you begin, then pause.
No, no. Better 'mudot.'

The man dressed as chaplain nods, gravely.
Write it down for me, please.
Let me see it on paper.

Casts about him for paper, a pencil,
in the manner of innocent interest.

You complete the translation
including several corrections
the more to appear convincing;

op raut jupitvo, it runs,
pevasen yonrai foyotonat,
q'sonat ommi,
rao op yiso dujpovopi duptotvov
neyoni pevasen evvopjov janepen.

You rub eyes, pinch forehead,
feign a translator's exhaustion.
Let me see, asks the chaplain
with just the right cadence
of innocent curiosity.

You push the paper across.
He gives it unhurried perusal,

murmurs a few words, a few phrases,
For the taste of the language, he says.

You coach his articulation
for five tentative minutes.

May he borrow the paper?
His collar is threadbare, his cuff stained.

You've no cause to suspect cunning.

XXII BABELBABBLE

The regiment's gone crazy.
Private Wolters' platoon
last night started speaking in tongues,

the effect, no doubt, of strong drink.
It sounded like conversation,

could be sounded in different ways
exemplygratier in bewilderment:-

Wolt: *Buzz. Guh?*
Hend: *Coffa buz.Ga?*

Wolt: *Crock.Crockty. Coroza.*
oraliter as incitement:-

Hend: *Buzz! Guh!*
Wolt: *Coffa BUZ ga!*

Hend: *Corrockty! Corrickty! CorrrrroZA!*

You made quite a stir
when you croaked in your parrot voice
Wee eeseen mooie jongen?   [*Who's a pretty boy?*]

and punctuated the singing
of *Drei hout douven*   [*Three wood pigeons*]
with a fair imitation of wood pigeons.

Best was, *na dertien kroezen,*   [*after thirteeen tankards*]
you had them chanting
Onzen! Gret onzen!   [*Nonsense! Great nonsense!*]

Some of them came to blows.
Some of them wept in their beer.
It meant nothing at all.

XXIII *ANOTHER VERSION OF CICERO*

That translation you showed me three weeks ago,
says the plausible cleric—I am ashamed to confess
I have lost it. Wind, rain, the hazards of life in tents…

I wonder, would you be so kind?
If you can spare the time. If you would oblige.
If you smell danger, you don't show it.

If the manuscript's lost, there's no danger.
You're an obliging man.
He brings pencil and paper, more Cicero:-

Omnes enim trahimur et ducimur	*[For we are all attracted and drawn*
ad cognitionis et scientiae cupiditatem,	*to a desire for understanding and knowing,*
in qua excellere pulchrum putamus,	*in which we consider it glorious to excel,*
labiautem, errare, nescire, decipi,	*whereas to fall into error, to be ignorant, to be deceived,*
et malum et turpe ducimus.	*we consider both base and immoral.]*

You frown, as though searching
for a word, for the right word, and begin.
Unpit ipon vesjonas iv eadonas

ef duopuduit iv tevenuei darodotin,
op rae iydimmisi ramdsan ravenat,
meco estin, issesi, padesto, padesto……

It must not be too fluent.
You make a strategic pause.

But the cleric takes hold of the pencil,
Let me assist you, he says,

writing *meco estin, issesi, <u>pitdosi</u>*
<u>*fidoro iv neman iv vasri fadonat.*</u>

Your eyes meet over the paper.
Somewhere in the camp there are drumbeats.

Still looking you in the eye
the reverend murmurs

Sunt hic etiam sua praemia fraudi,
proffers a handshake.

You grasp his hand in your own.
You have understood perfectly.

XXIV *A PARTNERSHIP, THEN*

How it was fashioned
in the privacy of a tent
that bordered on secrecy
must remain undisclosed.

The regiment is drawn up,
at its head, Colonel Lauder;
Reverend Innes has made an effort.
This is not your first conversion.

Old names must be thrown away
—*Satoshi, Satoru*—
and new ones be given;
George, after the Colonel,

Shalmanser, after the king
of Assyria, scourge
of the Israelites, scourge
of the Ten Lost Tribes.

Water floods your forehead,
the trickle and splash
of all that renews,
of all that proclaims a fresh start.

Do *you believe*, he asks,
do you believe?
I do, you reply.

I do.

XXV   ULTERIOR MOTIVES

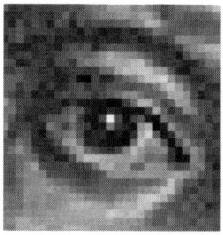

Alone in his tent, he does his best to conceal
the Great Hope that he has from the Watcher
who, knowing it, knows how far he is flawed.

His end is salvation, both of himself and others,
his hope of preferment a suggestion, no more,
of smoke from a smouldering thorn bush.

He cannot extinguish it. He hides it beneath
a blanket of pious endeavour, conspiratorial
in only the best interest of others. Some days,

washing his hands in a basin of *Scheldewater*
drawn from a chipped and dented enamel jug,
he believes himself truly free of it, truly free.

XXVI ULTERIOR MOTIVES (II)

What did we speak before Babel?
Is that what consumes you?
All later speech has deformed it.

Supposing the Protopalaver
the *ur-Sprache* of Eden,
might by converse deformations

of our wayward vernaculars
be rediscovered, the one and only
lost needle in language's haystack,

the deformations to find it
opaque to the wisest scholars
in the academy of projectors.

Is that the prize you imagine
beyond the truefalse parollfuddles
you hoodwink monoglots with?

XXVII IN THE ERASMUSSTAD

A week's walking at least with the Rev. Minder
and now you've reached Rotterdam. What message
has Desiderius left you folded between the leaves
of his last-century Bible and a register of the ships
you might board this week or next for England?

Captain Brant's crew have been sinking beerstoops
on the deck of the *Narrenschiff;* the harbour is rocked
by shouts, fisticuffs, shanties, and in the quayside bars
of the world's end, Zoltheid the gay girl is entertaining
mortality with a lewd song. The Delphshafen waters

are crowded with houseboats, rafts, half-barrels spun
round in furious circles by revellers, a village fleet
here occupied by the deluded, but elsewhere, set afloat
on the plausible tides of the transforming imagination,
articulate, girt, like those found on Formosa.

XXVIII *NULLIUS IN VERBA*

It's the verital age. The Network
meets every month to review evidence
for the truthful assertion of *What Is*.

Petitioners stake their credentials,
the mixture of rumour, invention, hope,
falsehood, belief, wishful thinking

that veils, or is passed off as, discovery.
The Network will find them out.
Next month, on *Damen 9th*, it's your turn.

XXIX   *CHIMNEYS*

They cannot determine your accent.
It somewhat resembles High Dutch, they complain,
though you insist it's pure Formosan.

How is it, they ask, *you are fair-haired
and fair-skinned, being raised in the tropics?*
Your underground noble houses

have sheltered you from the sun.
*How long is Formosan twilight? How long
is your midsummer shadow? How deep*

does the sun light a Formosan chimney?
Formosan chimneys are elbowed
half a span from the flaunching; the flues,

like your answers, are dark, secret spaces,
admitting no charperers' sunlight.
You can blag your palabra perfectly.

XXX TONGUETWISTERS

Ignatius's agents infiltrate Externitsa
in the guise of carpenters, plumbers,
cooks, merchants, disclosers of figs.
Trust them? They're after your soul.

Father de Rode, forced to flee,
steals you away to Avignon
where Fathers Mumbo and Jumbo
thrash Latin prayers into you.

Miseremini mei you moan, palms
raw with caning. If that really is
flesh and blood on your tongue,
they've made you a cannibal.

Nomo Domo, Hokum Kokum,
Vero Loco, breathe incense,
Ningo Jingo, hum the lingo,
Dives Eves, all pretence.

Let the corpses of criminals
executed in Externitsa, cooked
over a slow fire, be considered
a feast fit for a king.

Père Fontaney, late out of China,
has discovered you have no Mandarin.
And Formosa's a Chinese outpost,
not Japanese, as you'd have it.

For his Pope, then, substitute yours,
Gnotoy Bonzo, first of that name;
have him prescribe human sacrifice,
six, twelve, eighteen thousand

boys, every year, their hearts
plucked to roast on a gridiron.
The Network eschews disgust,
merely checks the arithmetic.

How is the population maintained?
Polygamy may explain it.
You ask *Of two barbarous tribes,
which is the less barbarous?*

XXXI *AT EDEN-ON-THAMES*

You're at ease talking of *Camphor Laurels*
with the Botanical Bishop, who has no specimen
yet in his Fulham parklands, though he has planted
a *Black Walnut*, a *Cork Oak*, and an *American Magnolia*,
the first of its kind in Europe. *On Formosa,* you tell him,
*there are laurels a hundred feet high, their white flowers
filling the whole island with fragrance in springtime.*

He's convinced by your narratives of conversion,
your hair's breadth escape from the Jesuits
and the sleight-of-hand treacheries he himself helped
free his country from at the Revolution still worthy,
he says, of being called *Glorious*. Under the *Cork Oak*
bursting today with acorns, convergence is Protestant,
the tolerant mind, free of chains, that admits dissent.

In the library, later, you add a Formosan *Lord's Prayer*
to the Palace's Archive of Vernaculars—*Amy khatsada*
it runs, *nadakchion toye ant nadayi; Give us this day
our daily bread.* This is your halfpenny loaf set to rise
in the admiration of others, though invention, its yeast,
shields herself still from disclosure, even as you search
for truth in the Camphor Laurels and stay hungry.

XXXII *AT A CHRIST CHURCH DINNER*

Among powdered wigs, your mane of blond hair
has turned heads. Lavinia, to your left, has
flushed cheeks and a white bosom that heaves
as she quizzes you, short of breath, about
Formosan notions of pastoral, while Kala
to your right, is aroused as much by the tang
of your alien idiolect as by what you can tell her
of *Chom*, *Hom*, *Porello* and *Chorche Matchin*.

They purport to be shepherdesses, searching,
perhaps, for the Tityrus you are not. Or perhaps
having already found, in the pastures of Other,
their metaphor of the possible, nurture yours.
The foundation of life is *invention*—all else
only its servile mimesis; Kala understands this,
Lavinia too, *Bajanes* both, now you spin them
a novel, outlandish form of the verb *to love*.

The Drinking Dean, opposite, is an inventor too.
He has drawn up a *Treatise on Architecture,* plans
for a new church, a new quadrangle. Like him,
you must sound, map and proportion your almost
perfected foundations, if they are to become
the public space you envisage. *Opportunity* edges
her door open, smiles, beckons you in. Your *Amen*
at the end of tonight's Grace was sincerely uttered.

XXXIII *THE ART OF FICTION*

⌋ ⌈ I ᓗ △ ᑫ

Somewhere, in our recalled fragments
of dream, argument, conversation,
there's the beginning all narratives have;

a time, a location, and someone
who might be authentic or figment
either dying, being born, or giving birth;

that event lodged in the imagination
and glimpsed through the glacial shifts
of the narrator-to-be's growing older,

or, magma like, bursting out of it
in a shower of catastrophe, spilling fire,
ash, devastation, narrative consequence.

My metaphor is the glacier, my glimpse
thirty years past of your experiments
gouging up gravel accumulations

that now I've gone grey coalesce
in the terminal moraine of this verse;
yours, the molten extravagance

of a life that would not be repressed
by doctrine or education but defined
itself in the fire of an imagining

that as I write marks our convergence.
I imagine you sitting upright all night
at the top of a draughty staircase,

devising, as I in a later age devise you
in this act of elaboration, the profile
of *Pacando*'s five islands, as credibly

named the *Peorkos*, *Little* and *Great*,
Thieves Islands, *Kaboski*, in your palabra
as *Orchid*, *Great Turtle*, *Green*, *Lamay*,

Formosa in mine. I see you wrapped
night after night at your writing desk
on which a candle is burning; you take

a drop or two of laudanum to keep
out the cold, keep you going, and page
after page, the fiction of your imagining

turns to document at your elbow.
Three hundred years later, I'm struck
by your gift for the plausible—six cities

named, and distinguished from towns
by the fact of their being walled, laws,
clothes, customs, beliefs, food, drink,

currency, festivals, titles, ranks, numbers
all granted their foothold, all grounded,
all grounding the names you give them,

so that, arriving at language, the lexis
of your Formosan, ripe with the true tang
of *difference*, offers itself as authentic

as the vernacular both of us forage in,
and I, who affirm nothing, lose myself
in a country no stranger than England,

picking my way through the labyrinth
of all that can be imagined, still at work,
still conjugating the verb *to explore*.

XXXIV POSTVERITAL (I) SILK

One day, selling cloth for your father
you went to the Isle of Robbers

and there in the Jarabut marketplace
you met Malaboska Bajane.

The Prison Governor's daughter,
she had come to buy wedding silks

watched over by armed guards
but held your eye long enough

for you to read anguish there
and manufacture a pretext

to visit her later in prison
with measures of shantung silk,

charmeuse, *habutai*. She called you
Saruto, her daybreak, spoke

of her captive life underground,
of a tyrannical, scheming father,

an arranged marriage; she dreamed
of escape to Pacando, a new life

with you, if not in Externitsa,
then wherever she might be free.

You planned your elopement,
but the Governor intervened,

brought forward her wedding day,
and expelled you from Jarabut,

set the dogs of revenge on your heels
until Father de Rode took you

into his protection, bringing you
to the mainland, to the Philippines,

to Goa, to Spanish *Gibralter, Thoulon,
Marseils, Aix,* finally *Avignon*

as set down in your *Travels*. Your state
changed from fugitive to itinerant,

to enquirer, philosopher, polyglot,
the founder-confounder of a new tongue

that brought fame and notoriety
to you in equal measures; no doubt

the exigencies of survival, invention,
earning a living, in time came to erode

the particulars of all you experienced
on the Isle of Robbers, but sometimes,

when thought was suspended, and light
fell in a sudden shaft on shot silk,

a woman came into your mind, her face
lifted in sunlight under a market awning

towards you, her eyes brown, unblinking
and you imagined it might be her.

*

It's three hundred years since you left
and Kannon has returned to Taiwan.

The prisons built after the massacre
that began the White Terror are gone;

they've become theatre, exhibition hall,
Museum of Witness, constituents

of a great Human Rights Memorial Park
where people come in their thousands

to remember oppression's victims
and with a poem, a prayer, or a kind word

affirm peace, freedom, compassion.
Today almost two million people stand

in a five hundred kilometre line
from the north to the south of Big Island;

at 2.28pm they take hold
of their neighbours' hands and declare

Love Peace, Say No to Weapons,
while on Green Island, the park's

full to bursting with pacifists, travellers,
ecotourists, a multicultural space,

inclusive, full of hope, full of love.
Notes fall from guitars, weed burns;

in the Cave of Kannon, there is
a stalactite shaped like a woman,

her hips bound with red silk;
my life at its core, beyond true and false,

is shaped by imagining; seeing this,
it's to her I stretch out my hand.

XXXV POSTVERITAL
(II) TWO VERBS FROM FORMOSA

The verb *to love* in Formosan is *chato*.
I love is translated *Jerh chato*, the two
syllables of the verb keeping a level tone.

The preterite, *I loved*, and the future, *I shall love*,
employ the same two words, the verb spoken
with a falling and with a rising tone respectively.

The imperfect, *I was loving*, requires
the auxiliary verb *vieye* to be added,
and a level tone used in delivery.

The pluperfect, *I had loved*, is formed
with the same auxiliary but is delivered
with a falling tone, like the preterite.

The future perfect, *I shall have loved*, uses
the auxiliary verb *viar*, and like the future
is pronounced with a rising tone.

Note that the Japanese, speaking Formosan, make
the last syllable of the auxiliary a verb suffix
and ignore all distinctions of tone.

*

In Mandarin, *lingua franca*
of modern Taiwan, *qipian*
is the verb *to deceive*.

Its present tense, *I deceive*,
is *wo qipian*, the verb element spoken
with a low dipping tone.

The future, *I shall deceive,*
has the auxiliary *hui* and is also delivered
with a low dipping tone.

The imperfect, *I was deceiving,* adds
the auxiliary *bei* and is pronounced
with a mid rising tone.

I shall have deceived, future perfect,
adds both previous auxiliaries,
pronounced with a high falling tone.

The preterite, *I deceived,*
is *wo qipianle,* pronounced
with a mid rising tone.

Note that the Taiwanese cherish *kuso,*
trash internet games, practical jokes, hoaxes that end
Wo quipianle nimen: *I have deceived you all.*

XXXVI POSTVERITAL   (III) BAMBOO

Wanting to purge your mind
of dogma, deponent verbs, and the dull
thud of the fourth declension,

you slip out of Externitsa
one day while Father de Rode
is lost in his genuflexions,

walk northwards for five days
and reach Basianshan on the sixth.
Its forest of bamboo groves

are those of the mind, from which
an imagining shoot, uncurling, pushes
towards sunlight and expression.

About you, young thickets dance
as the wind blows, whisper their thoughts
in a language you have yet to learn;

older ones rattle the stems
of their neighbours, so your thoughts dance
to percussive music, or quarry

a pulse you cannot predict
but let quicken your tongue to a new speech
alien at first, even to you that speak it.

You breathe, rustle, sough vowels;
tongue, palate, teeth, lips shape consonant clatter,
the dynamic of diphthongs, until

at dawn on the seventh day,
you are enlightened by sense. The new language
is yours, the thoughtprint and mark

of your fabrication; your mind,
born afresh to itself hourly in renewed acts
of imagining, at one with

bamboo's clumping and running,
its rampant proliferation, its single mass flowering
after a long interval, in accordance

with the laws of prime numbers.
You turn back to Externitsa and its humdrum
of inflexion and conjugation,

hollow-hearted, compassionate,
the coils of inventive thought set to prosper
when grounded in daily occurrence.

Father de Rode upbraids you, presses
for the confession you recite, or do not recite.
You don't disclose where you've been.

*

Fifty miles to the south, and three centuries later,
Grandmaster Wei Chueh founds a monastery;
its precepts, respect for one's elders, kindness

towards the young, harmony with all humanity,
and truth in all one's endeavours. One day
the Grandmaster points to a spray of silk orchids

flecked with glass water drops. He asks a monk
Are the water drops false, or authentic? The monk
answers *They are artificial, Grandmaster.*

Three times, the Grandmaster asks
Are the water drops false, or authentic?
Three times, the monk gives his answer;

The droplets are not genuine, Grandmaster.
Then the Grandmaster smiles and remarks
They are faked to look real. Months or years later

the monk learns from the Grandmaster's teaching
how deftly cognition trapped him
in the trammels of *either…or*. What's artificial

—the droplets, the Grandmaster's question—
may be a gateway to truth, the monk's, as the poet's
duty, to persevere in his calling. He has turned

their exchange over and over, neglected,
recalled it, turned it over again until realisation
comes to him, the fall of rain on an orchid.

XXXVII *POSTVERITAL*
(IV) THE MAXIM OF AFFIRMATION

Whatever they say of Formosa
you claim is mere happenstance;
Chinese may have been spoken

on the coastline of contradiction
and women there given birth
before they were thirty-six

but *Formosa exterior* gives few clues
to an interior never explored
by trustworthy witnesses, a dark

centre where falsehood and truth,
obedient both to the laws
of the feigning imagination,

shake hands in uneasy peace.
Let superintendent Kings here
rule subject to Edo; let none here

be a mother before she is forty;
here let Formosan be spoken.
This centre of supposition

is shaped from your affirmations,
a locus in which the sensational
is sustained by the plausible,

its astonishments underpinned
by a thousand particulars
supportive of one another

as each tongue, Formosan included,
fashions the polyglot world
we quarrel and misunderstand in.

So you admit no retraction
preferring to spin a new line
when the fabric runs threadbare,

adding colour, circumstance,
substance to turn disbelief
into credit, *Formosa interior*

less a place than a state of mind
where the imagined occurs
with the full force of reality.

*

How should my predicates
ill-formed and mendacious
today claim to be different?

These lines of entanglement
cannot attain but point to
a *Terra Damnata* resonant

not with what is, but what may be,
an undiscovered interior
that the ranging imagination

triangulates without guile
in stanzas that celebrate
albeit in current language

the rumour and parle of perhaps,
and, visiting, shapes its fictions
of what may be worth credit.

XXXVIII *DE LIBRO SUO*

You might have written your book
in Formosan, but the readers
of Externitsa would have had
no interest in its contents,
and no-one in Western Europe
understands a word of the language.

Better, therefore, to have written
your description in Latin,
the *lingua franca* of Europe,
and indeed of the civilised world
—an *ur-text* for every vernacular
you would have it translated into.

And here come the translators already,
the ink scarcely dry on your last page
—the man you call *Dr Oswald,* a Scots
man of the cloth, who might pass
in a poor light for Rev Minder,
and a French scholar, camouflaged

as *le Sieur N.F.D.B.R.,* who may be
your *alter ego* (he claims in his preface
to have enjoyed daily discussions
of nuance and equivalence with
the work's author) or may indeed be
the *Nicolas François Du Bois Refugie*

that, setting misinformation right
in a later work, you say he is.
The selves that you are proliferate
amid ever diminishing fractals,
the Dutch text transposing
the majuscules *D* and *B* so that

the ghost of Father *de Rode* appears
once again in your history, linking you,
or your translator, at three removes,
with Rodez perhaps, in Gascony,
with Aveyron for Avignon, with what
never occurred, with what happened.

I visited Rodez once, on a June day
when the city was packed with pilgrims.
The immense redbrick cathedral
boomed with Latin, French, Occitan.
A doorkeeper proffered an alms dish;
there was no sign of you anywhere.

XXXIX *INVENTIONS*

From the centre, your life moves towards margin.
Last winter, Fame blew Formosan fanfares
on her brazen trumpet, and coffee house talk
dissected your latest lecture; controversy
fuelled The Network's exchanges, and centres

of learning reckoned themselves ignorant
had they not your acquaintance. But Fame, lately,
has been blowing her trumpet elsewhere;
Dr Oswald has won promotion, and now cares
for battalions in Portugal while few trouble

themselves these days to defend, to refute,
or even explore your particulars. A cold wind
blows you from Christ Church to Grub Street,
the drudge end of the pen-pushing universe
where you must scratch out new ways of living.

I imagine you one winter's day, as snow covers
the roof of your copyists' garret, taking twelve
drops of laudanum to keep out the cold; a vision
of Externitsa gives way to an echo of Babel,
shouts from the street outside, where someone

is calling you in a tongue reminiscent of Hebrew.
Shin Aleph Lamed he calls, *Shin Aleph Lamed
Mem Nun Zayin* all the way along Grub Street.
Three centuries pass, or time makes a standstill
as you look out into the street, ready to answer

but the street is deserted, a thoroughfare lost
in its own apprehensions as I too am dissolved
in these inventions, a handful of letters spilled
in straight lines over my notebooks, among which
I walk in amazement, a traveller finding his way.

XL *A DISCOURSE FROM SERVITUDE*

What happens to time? Somewhere high in the hills
ostents fall onto rocks shaped over millennia;
they gather and trickle, gouge channels that run

into climate and season, meandering, driving,
now in flood, now so still that our willow thought
hangs motionless in their reaches. Experience, once

overrunning invention so fast that years passed
in the blink of an eye, here turns to accretion,
the slow saturation of mind in its contemplations

whether yours, in the mining of Hebrew, or mine,
in unravelling truth from what passes for truth
in your conjuror's sleeve of falsehood. Meanwhile

we must both of us make a living. Once I sold prints
from a stall on a London street, once polished floors
for rich Hampstead housewives, spent my strength

digging footings on building sites, taught the young
and the not so young how poetry frees the mind
from self-sufficiency's chains, as it still frees my own;

you write puffs for enamelware, balance accounts
for a regiment, teach Latin, fortress design, paint fans
as I once hand-coloured those prints, our time costed

at so many shillings an hour. Deep under the trammels
of what it takes to survive, a beaker of laudanum
summons up Shalmaneser, King of Assyria, predator

on Israel and Egypt alike, deporter of the Lost Tribes.
His face is a mask, his snake tongue a hieroglyph
spread between berm lips parched by the centuries,

his voice when he speaks the dry, whispering rasp
of desert sand blasting an obelisk. Not even Formosa
heard syllables such as these, raw, incomprehensible,

to *Gomera Pedlo Samdo,* fugitive, polymath, outcast
in the City of Ur which he once thought was London,
a prospector of languages found guilty of forgery

and sentenced to hard labour, who as the vision fades
comes to himself in his cell, thirsty and unrepentant,
the Assyrian's name on his lips consonant with his own.

XLI *A FAN SHOP, 1717*

In the back room of a fan shop you've been dipping
squirrel hair into pots of pigment. The templates
for your designs exist in an imagination charged

only now and again with tincture of laudanum,
pronunciation of *The Name*, or of certain syllables
from the Hebrew which you're now exploring.

Old Testament patriarchs visit you after midnight,
making their way past drying trays spread with leaves
depicting your vanities, which day-men tomorrow

will assemble with ribbing, guardsticks and rivets
into the finished product. Abraham is impatient
with your representations of sacrifice, Noah chafes

at Formosan fauna never seen boarding his ark.
Moses stands by the Commandments, his finger
outstretched in reprimand to point at the ninth,

which his gesture makes clear you've infringed.
They proclaim your offences in Hebrew; you submit
to their reproofs in the belief you may be no more

than a breath-point or a consonant shift from
the *ur sprache*, but the bread of deceit has leavened
your tongue for so long you can ask no favours

and their mouths are too full of gravel to condescend.
Besides, it's turned cold; the time's right not for questions
nor repentance, but for more opium, which you take.

Somewhere a lamb bleats, somewhere a light burns;
the Thames, down from Ludgate Hill, joins and divides.
Dawn comes. None of the patriarchs buys a fan.

XLII *AUTOBIOGRAPHY, 2017*

It's fifty years, give or take,
since your scabby hand plucked my sleeve
in a basement off Baker Street

and reading one version
of the part-story you told, I saw for the first time
how substitution of names

might free my imagination
from the cage of its everyday, the woman
I now know as Jeanne du Moment

setting me down with my pencil
and bidding me map the moon. She placed
this world and others before me

saying *Draw what you imagine*
which since then I have always considered
a transpersonal duty, content

that *invention* should sometimes
signify what I found and at other times be
what I invented, *a fabrication*,

some said, or more kindly,
the work of devising mind. Peter Ramus,
my flatmate, one day brought home

a rucksack stuffed full of manuals
on logic, rhetoric, grammar he'd picked up
from a fleamarket in Bloomsbury

—Quintilian, Seneca, Cicero—a joblot
of lenses, he said, for working my poetry through.
I set them out on my desk, visited

similarity, difference, cause, effect,
consequence, antecedent, before, during, after,
wherever Invention lay sleeping

for Jeanne and the poet I was to bring
focus and words to arouse her. Years passed,
our efforts perspectived in the pages

of newspapers, magazines, pamphlets,
slim volumes, most of all in computer files
labelled *Unpublished Verses,* enlarged

almost daily, all marking our passage,
some giving pleasure to others, all premised
on the free play of the imagination

unharnessed except to such truth
as it believed it might make its own. This leads me,
thirty years on, to a point on my journey

where, having acquainted myself
through diligence and my own acts of imagining
 with your history of Formosa,

I confront your retraction, and my road forks,
becoming one way a wide boulevard of acceptance
where I take your remorse at face value

and dissolve as you do into platitudes,
the other a tortuous thorn path littered with skulls
along which, barefoot and incredulous,

I may inch my way through the gloaming
and snared in discredit, my glib lack of judgement,
lose all sense of direction.

Why did you compose your retraction
over twenty or thirty years, adding a few sheets
on odd Wednesdays and Fridays

to a deep drawer on the right hand side
of your white cabinet, to be found after your death
but not published during your lifetime?

Could this be a fiction in progress?
a dark work of contriving mind? an experiment?
a sublime egotistical act of *Maybe*?

Why make your will and confirm it
ten years afterwards, yet have neither document
name truly the man you were?

The man who became Newgate chaplain
and heard among others the scaffold confession
of Dr Dodds, knew you well; he said

you spoke French *far beyond
what might be attained by grammar and travel only*,
moreover that you were *a master*

*of the Gascoin dialect in particular,
so hard for foreigners to speak with propriety, fluency,
vivacity, that you must have been born*

in some part of Languedoc. But you kept
yourself from him and from all of us, an invented man
to the last, as poetry (that sublime form

of lying) invents those who write it.
The fork in the road, Jeanne du Moment advises,
is the falsehood of *either, or*;

both the boulevard and the footpath
lead to the same destination—short term, your decease,
three hundred years later, the last line

of these verses of exploration. *Draw
what you imagine* she urges; *the dust of our journey
together gives you canvas enough.*

I go back to the fan shop to find you
but a sign in the doorway reads *Business Closed*
and the windows display only dead flies.

Biding my time, at nightfall I break in,
make my way to your work desk in a squalid back room
filmy with cobwebs. The floor's littered

with the peel of Seville oranges, the top
of your desk a waste land of cancelled proofs,
torn strips of paper, smudged sketches,

among these some hexagrams, struts
thickened in places, forming a varied shape repertoire
within the one standard framework.

Mystified for a moment, I decipher
the Star of David; within it, densely inked forms
of the Hebrew alphabet, among which

Gimel, Pe, Samech are predominant. Voices
call from the street; now I can see where you're going.
I can see my own way ahead.

XLIII *BREATHING SPACE*

Rev Ploughshare has raised you a stipend
from his generous congregation.

Give what you can he urged; *free
a devout Asian convert from the drudgery*

*that is beneath him. Give
him the means to study divinity.*

The response has been
magnificent—twenty-three pounds last year,

twenty-seven this, more than enough
for food, rent, books, paper, laudanum.

You make an effort with manuals
of devotion, Hebrew grammars,

the Pentateuch, *Kings, Joshua, Judges,*
draft essays to help a young

inexperienced country clergyman
win arguments with unbelievers.

The gift brings you breathing space
but neither Asian nor convert you're uneasy

at a life grounded on falsehood.
At least, so your *Memoirs* say.

XLIV DISENGAGEMENT

Your only vice these days is laudanum
and you live alone for the most part

except when the patriarchs come
with their holy eyes and grey beards

mistaking you sometimes for their own.
A conversation with Moses

brings darkness for several days,
a plague of frogs in your bedroom;

a visit from Joshua, the echo
of distant trumpets, stones falling

from London Wall, and the clatter
of Rahab's heels on the pavement.

Tonight David calls, bringing
not Jonathan, not Bathsheba,

but his *kinnor* and a book of psalms.
He sings you the sixty-third

his beautiful voice filling your room
with its resonant tenor;

what should you do but join him
in a thirsty land without water,

a wilderness full of thorns
where it's hard to stay upright?

XLV MASTERING HEBREW

נ פ ס א ל ם

(i) Reading

You can distinguish the letter forms—tell the hook,
Vau, from *Zayin*, the weapon; read the *tfel ot thgir*
words with their vowel points on the printed page,
know which letters are servile, which radical,
but the grammars exhaust your patience.

Better a Hebrew text of the Psalms, with the Latin
set out on the facing page. Pagninus delivers
the word-for-word sense in Latin, John Leusden
their Hebrew original; with the help of a Lexicon
you grasp idiom, nuance, over repeated readings.

You conjugate, err, and correct, murmur words
off the page with the best guess you can manage.
Their texture is that of stoned fruit, apricots,
olives perhaps, their taste sweet, their fragrance
more subtle even than that of your old Formosan.

(ii) The pronunciation of Hebrew

In the Portuguese Synagogue you listen to psalms
sung in the Sephardic tradition. What you hear
is a Hebrew refracted through two millennia
of the Lisbon and London vernaculars, a distinct
sociolect incomprehensible when you attempt

conversation in Hebrew with elders. Your accent
is guesswork, theirs a mutated hotchpotch.
The Moroccans, however, grounded in Arabic,

find your Hebrew intelligible. Did words of three
consonants only comprise the world before Babel?

You read and recite the psalms over and over.
From them you build your wordstock, enlarging,
refining; the tireless play of the mind discovering
through study, the fruits of creative abundance.
Once you can speak Hebrew, you can think in it.

(iii)   Writing

In your white cabinet, they'll find manuscript notes
of your writings in Hebrew—an unfinished verse
tragi-comedy featuring *David and Michal,* drafts
of a *Dialogue between a Jew and a Christian
concerning the Second Coming*; also, I imagine,

texts too slight to be named in your *Memoirs*.
It's hard now they've been lost to determine
whether your Englished Psalms were more just
than Bishop Hare's, which you call *a poor, low,
crawling humdrum bitony of trochaics and iambics,*

or vice versa, as readers may please, or whether
you're piqued at his having hijacked your publisher.
After we're gone, what becomes of the experiments
we found wanting, shelved, and meant to get back to
stacked in a white cabinet or uploaded to Dropbox?

XLVI   THE ANTICHTHON EXPEDITION

In the Antichthon I imagined, words were things;
I travelled there in a ship named *The Projector,*
its captain one Lesauvage, a native of Amsterdam.

His daughter, Jeanette, was pilot and navigator;
she had a good ear for music and a nose for adventure.
What winds blew us off track and what adverse currents

hampered our course through *The Narrows,* I can't tell
but we struck land in the April of '64, and stayed there
more than a twelvemonth, with pickaxes, dynamite,

splitting open the word-globes that littered the plain.
Their surfaces, rough or smooth, hid compressed strata
of all human history, which we extracted, disfigured

somewhat by explosives, and packed in shrink wrap
to bring home for analysis. We stored these in *Lonzep,*
the capital, in a rented warehouse, where we received

in the course of the year, delegations of visitors
from the Academies of Yedo, Lagado, Taipei, all eager
to examine our residues and in some cases to formulate

theories of their significance. The earthquake that struck
in the August of '65 and destroyed the whole island
gave us no time to salvage our findings; we were lucky

indeed to have time to relaunch *The Projector,* ride out
the aftershocks, and sail out of range with our lives.
Of Antichthon, nothing remained. Jeanetta suggested

I write what I remembered, and so, on the voyage home,
on my return to England, and when inspiration combined
ever after with opportunity, I have compiled the verses

of which these, the most recent, are the latest survivors
of the Antichthon landscape, plucked out of the ground
of imagination, truth-flecked, solid as stone, light as air.

XLVII *INTIMATIONS*

Every third day the fever prostrates you,
a malarial cold that chills to the marrow;
I wake in the small hours, fog in my left eye.

Gervase, your friend, brings you posset ale
with an infusion of dandelion; I'm prescribed
daily doses of statins, clopidogrel.

You shake, shudder and the sweat runs.
The cardiologist in the echo room checks
the gurgle and swish of my blood.

What should we do, glimpsing mortality,
but with reading and meditation shore up
our spirit's uncertain foundations?

You answer Law's *Serious Call to a Devout
and Holy Life*; I swing on the gateless gate,
thumbs touching, sit down on the blue cliff.

You begin your confessions– a few pages
a day, setting the record straight; I resume
my daily work of devising. We accumulate

and discard, practise our arts of adjustment,
though you can know nothing of me, and I
of you only what circumstance has let fall

for these paperchase verses. I shape them
in a spirit of exploration, trusting my own
skill in invention no more than I trust yours.

XLVIII   *MANAGING HISTORY*

You sit in your Old Street lodgings, writing histories.

For Samuel Palmer, Printer, deceased,
there's the last third of his *History of Printing*
from its invention in Mentz to its spread
throughout Europe, and notably England.
You claim to have authored the whole thing
from some dozen sources. No one else has
your grasp of significance, detail, perspective.

For the Booksellers' Collective, it's *The History
of the Jews* from the time of Abraham
to the destruction of Solomon's temple,
and beyond, down to the present.
They've appointed you Project Manager
of the *Universal History* yours is part of;
you'll not live to see its completion.

For yourself, there's the accumulation
of a revised autobiography—the true,
frank and authentic confession of forgery,
misrepresentation, repentance. You write
in a scholarly English, full of connectives;
this is what history is—the congruence,
over time, of individual fortunes.

On my laptop, a search engine displays
your Paternoster Row writings. I can see
at their core the work of enquiring mind,
adaptive, meticulous, vigorous as bamboo
in the groves of Basianshan you imagined
half a lifetime ago, as I did, their twisting,
tormented tendrils reaching to speech.

XLIX THREE WOMEN

(i)

A few yards of silk bring her back to you
even now from the Jarabut market place
where, long since, I imagined you meeting.

Has she gone grey in the interval? Has she
lost her magic, not at all the same thing?
Or, ripened with love, is she still mistress

of the improvised verse that each morning
opened the doors of your heart? Unchanged
in your memory, how should she know you,

a penitent, elderly scholar with bad teeth
and a laudanum habit, scratching a living,
for the maker of fables you once were?

(ii)

You gave them up for your books, all but one,
a liaison you term *rather trifling than culpable*.

From the hall of oblivion, a voice challenges
Trifling? Culpable? Aren't they the same thing?

(iii)

I imagine her, unmarried, in her mid forties,
(a Sarah Rewalling was christened in 1702)
preparing a light supper in Ironmonger Row;

she's cleared the table of papers, set bread,
milk, ends of cold chicken, and now stands,
by your chair, head bowed, ready to serve.

A good friend, worthy and pious, she's laid
radishes by your trencher, their crimson skins
damp from their ewer dowsing; you can't say

you're not tempted. The tester next-door's
overloaded with books loaned for the *History*,
but with her help you might just make room.

L *LAUDANUM*

You drink tea in the daytime, take six drops
of laudanum at night in a pint of small punch

and as you approach seventy, are grateful.
It has prevented decay of your spirits

through senility, close study, a life spent
without exercise, reading and writing,

and you've learned to control your intake
from the vainglory days of ten tablespoons

morning and night, though a cold winter
now and again has brought fluctuations.

Who knows whether Sydenham's tincture
fuelled your trips to Formosa, or whether

coming to consciousness there, you found
only laudanum could give you the strength

to describe what you'd seen? Imagination,
rife in her assumings, redeems and betrays;

seeing substance and shadow are one,
her workings transcend truth and falsehood

like that rain on the Grandmaster's orchid
or the footsteps of those we hear walking

all day through the decision maze of the self
and acknowledge tonight are our own.

LI *AN INTERNET JOURNEY*

The distinction you draw in your *Memoirs*
between *servile* and *radical* letters
directs me to my search engine.
I embark on a long, distant journey,

travel backwards and forwards in time
via *A Hebrew Manual for Beginners,*
to an account of mnemonic formulae
for differentiating the letters.

The formulae were devised by Saadia
ben Joseph of Egypt, author of The *Agron,*
a lost treatise on words, in the tenth century.
The twenty-two letters are sequenced

in two groups of eleven, comprising
a single, dense, enigmatic sentence
that might be translated *Thus (in the same
manner that I composed the Agron) did*

Abraham write a book on the true roots.
I search for Abraham's book, discover
Sefer Jezirah, the *Book of Formation;*
this too is accessible, and I visit it.

It deals with creation, the coming about
of the whole world of things and ideas
from the ten primary numbers
and the twenty two letters of Hebrew,

among these, the three serviles
Aleph, Mem, Shin being pre-eminent.
My journey has brought me to a new
sense of your imagined Formosan

and the English I treat as authentic;
their lexicon, grammar, articulation
all sprung from a common root,
from breath, the combustive spirit,

the material tug of form that confers
substance to thought, validates art,
and gives life to all that's imagined.
Is it possible that your Formosan

having led you to learning Hebrew
could have led you to share the same
Cabbalistic suspicions that I have?
I come back to our manuscripts

and start searching for congruence
but there is none. On the same page,
you dismiss Munster's annotations
to his first Hebrew Bible, which

you say, being *of the Massoretic
or Cabbalistical kind, would rather
clog than assist*. I'm not inclined
towards mysticism either, though

I prefer what links to what separates,
what's imagined to boastful truth
or shamed falsehood, the dreamer's
and the poet's rare gift of supposing.

LII *INHERITANCE*

For her there are your books, clothes, household goods,
your money, such as it is, and your manuscripts.
Perhaps, before breathing your last, you bequeathed her
your birth name, though your will never states it.

For posterity there are the narratives of a life built on fiction
that reformed itself into fact, the chancer turned penitent,
the forged man who renounced his deception, the hoodwink
adventurer ransomed by scholarly histories.

For me, there are the many thousand shifts of envisaging
that occasioned these half hundred verses, the precipitate
of mouse click and library hours that offer no certainties
but transform us to parts of speech leaving Formosa.